PUPS PAWS ON WHEELS

Written by
Jessica Heaton

Illustrated by
Mikey Shiraz Baird

© Pups On Wheels, 2020

First published in 2020

Written By Jessica Heaton

Illustrations: Mikey Shiraz Baird (mikey@parishpub.co.uk)

Interior Layout and Design: Bryony van der Merwe (bryonyvdmerwe@gmail.com)

ISBN: 978-1-8382141-0-4 (paperback edition)
ISBN: 978-1-838221141-1-1 (electronic edition)

Published by:
Pups On Wheels
info@pupspawsonwheels.com

I would like to thank
Salima Kadaoui, Sally,
for changing the lives of many
animals in Tangier, Morocco. Her
hard work and dedication inspired me
when writing this book.

8 a.m.

It's breakfast time in the puppy sanctuary. Pups are hopping around as I scoop biscuits into bowls.

Hungry fur-babies, **big and small, shuffle and bounce** their way towards me.

If it wasn't for the soft sand, they'd have sores on their legs. You see, they can't use all four legs to stand, run, and play like the others.

Yama is trying to steal other puppies' food.

Luckily, I'm there to stop her.

"No, Yama!"

9 a.m.

I clean up the sandpit and sit down,
ready for cuddles.

Hayat is first. What a lot of pups ready for a kiss!

"I love you all."

Big, bright eyes stare at me, shining with joy as I start putting each pup in the wheelchair specially made for them.

Strapped in safely, out of the sandpit they go. Lucky leads the way into the open grounds.

"Enjoy your exercise, guys!"

The pups fly through the door, knocking into each other like dodgems at the fairground.

10 a.m.

Sahara is desperate to keep up with the others.
Sooty is biting one of Lucky's wheels.
It's my job to rescue everyone.

Hercules comes to help!

I hear banging, and look there's Cesar crashing into a doorway, trying to get some leftover doggie biscuits he's spotted.

"Cesar, if you eat too much, you'll be too full to run around again later," I tell him.

Cesar doesn't listen.

"Right. I think it's chill-out time,"
I tell him as I pick up his lead.

11 a.m.

Cesar and Theo can't shuffle or hop around like the other puppies, so I put nappies on them.

I carefully tuck them around their bellies near their back legs so everything is tidy.

"We don't want any accidents, do we, boys?" I say.

12 noon

The pups rush over to see Bluebell.

She is not always very friendly!

I call the pups away, and they all start to follow me. Speedy Sam rolls over my feet with his big rubber wheels, bashing into my side to get closer to me.

Yama and Sooty are on my other side, doing the same.

"Hey! I can't move," I shout.

I throw a ball for them to fetch, and Lucky and Sooty zoom ahead. Yama races after them, nipping and nibbling at them to get their attention.

"Yama, no!" She stops and gives me a sweet, innocent look but then starts again.

"Cheeky Yama!"

1 p.m.

It's rest time. I open the sandpit gate, lift all the pups in and unclip them from their wheels.

But wait, someone is missing. Cassie just needs a **little extra help and reassurance.**

12

All the pups are sunbathing in the golden sand.

It's very hot.

"Are you thirsty, pups?" I say,
filling the water bucket to the very top.

 2 p.m

Two of the quieter pups, Sahara and Hayat, shuffle towards me. As I stroke them, they push themselves into me, asking for more.

Without cuddles and rest, the pups would be sad, lonely, and worn out.

Only happy, healthy pups here!

Sam rushes over and starts to play-fight a little too roughly.

"Time for you to go into your den with Yama," I say.

They snuggle up together, and Yama nibbles his ear with love.

Yama and Sam simply adore each other.

3 p.m.

Cesar's and Theo's ears are standing tall, and their eyes are extra bright. They want to go out again in their wheelchairs.

I take off their dirty nappies and open the gate.

"Freedom for the pups!"

4 p.m.

Daylight is fading and the sun's slowly starting to tuck itself to bed behind the big green hills that surround the sanctuary. Now it's time for the last run of the day.

Lucky and Sooty are fidgeting and fighting to get out the gate before I've had a chance to get them into their chairs.

"Cheeky pups!"

Holding Cassie up, I clip her into her harness and put her feet into the stirrups. She turns back, licking at my arm to say thank you.

"It's important you're comfortable and clipped in properly," I say.

5 p.m.

The towering, noisy red gates open, leading to the other end of the sanctuary.

The pups race through, **barging and bashing** into each other all the way.

Poor Hayat takes a tumble. I gently grab the sides of her chair and turn her back upright.

Off she zooms to join her friends.

"**Be careful!**" I shout.

6 p.m.

"Now then, who wants a snack and the **last lot of cuddles before bedtime?**" I say.

Sweet and small Sahara stands patiently, waiting at the back to get in for a snuggle. Picking her up and out of her chair, I place her on my knee.

"Can't have anyone left out now, can we?"

7 p.m.

The sun has almost disappeared.
The pups look at me, knowing it's bedtime.

"Bed, bed!" I shout, calling the pups to their sandpit.

It's getting cold now. I put coats on each pup. I give Sam **a blanket and an extra thick coat**. Sam hasn't got much fur to keep warm like the others.

24

The day has come to an end, and all pups are ready for bed. Going around, I give out kisses before everyone falls asleep.

I pull down the sandpit covers to keep them all warm and dry at night.

"Good night, fur-babies, sleep tight."

About The Author:
Jessica Heaton

Jessica Heaton, animal activist and international volunteer, was inspired to write this book when she saw the mistreatment of animals around the world and a lack of awareness of their needs. Thankfully, hope is created by those loving individuals who volunteer and run sanctuaries.

A very special sanctuary called SFT-Sanctuary of the Animals of Tangier, in Morocco, revealed to Jessica how happy a dog could be when they are loved, whether it has one leg or no legs at all. It was an experience Jessica wanted to share with others, especially children who may not understand about animals with disabilities, how to care for them and how they can live happily in safety. Now.

Currently working as an auxiliary nurse at a specialist orthopaedic and neurology referral hospital in the UK, Jessica sees many dogs and cats with neurological diseases and physical disabilities. They undergo physio sessions, rehab programmes and in some cases surgery, and this assists them to live a more positive life.

One of the most important things Jessica learnt from working with all kinds of animals around the world is that animals may not be able to speak to you or tell you how they feel, but they can certainly show it in their behaviour; a smile; a jump; a wriggle or a wag of a tail are all signs of joy.

Printed in Great Britain
by Amazon